ISBN 0 85079 140 5

TAK CARTOONS

FROM
THE STANDARD (LONDON)
&
THE DAILY EXPRESS

BOOK SIXTEEN

£1.35p

Thirteen British Leyland workers were sacked for making false statements on their application forms. BL said they were part of a Left-wing infiltration conspiracy.

"I think we can drop our suspicions about this one, sir. Judging by these results his three 'O' levels are forgeries!"

A Pakistani gentleman arrived at Heathrow with a passport showing his age as 159. An airline official said he didn't look a day over 140.

"Now we'll settle how old he is—here comes his dad!"

"The committee's had a complaint about your keel too!"

The America's Cup trials and the Americans were
highly suspicious of design modifications; sadly, Peter de Savary's
Victory 83 didn't make it to the challenge series.

An expert shocked the MCC by saying that many of the paintings in the Long Room at Lord's were fakes.

"I always thought it was a fake, it's nothing like Boycott's stance at the crease."

The headmaster of Dartington Hall School in Devon resigned and after he told parents about goings-on at the establishment he soon hit the headlines . . . more so when old nude pictures of him and his wife were published.

"HORACE! I should have thought you could have got the head's job on the strength of your academic achievements alone!"

The breathalyser gave way to a computerised test for drunken drivers but the technological marvel fell short of its infallible reputation. Not so reliable as those simple crystals . . .

"By the time we had worked out the technicalities of the print-out he was sober again."

Cockroaches were found in the Café Royal kitchen and a prosecution followed.

"Would madam kindly remove her beetle brooch? It's upsetting the sauce chef!"

US Navy ships shelled anti-government strongholds in the mountains behind Beirut, Druze artillery also opened fire and the American embassy was hit.

"Dammit, Elmer! Can't you claim diplomatic immunity or something?"

An inept England soccer team was beaten 1—0 by Denmark in a European Championship game at Wembley.

"Bring on the hooligans!"

" Keep going Jimmy, there's a man here from the Guinness Book of Records ! "

Celebrities galore in the Bob Hope charity golf
tournament but not everyone was in the Ballesteros class.

Lord Snowdon was temporarily blinded when two unknown men threw a liquid in his face when he was in a chauffeur-driven car.

"That's Norman Parkinson in the clear. Now let's see if Lord Lichfield and David Bailey have alibis!"

Australia won the America's Cup, a bitter blow for the exclusive New York Yacht Club where the trophy was bolted to a table.

What do we do now, appeal to the Supreme Court or take out a contract with The Mafia?

A dancer was sacked from the London Festival Ballet because he wasn't strong enough to lift ballerinas.

"Well, that's manly enough. dear. Now could we try it without your handbag?"

"We can relax now Sid, the law's caught up with him!"

A retired firearms dealer heard intruders next door and fired five shots into the ground—after calling on them to stop as they were leaving. One bullet ricocheted and hit one of the men in the leg. He successfully sued for damages, but sympathisers raised the money.

An alien spacecraft was said to have landed in a clearing in a Suffolk forest at Christmas, 1980. Locals, including airmen from a US base nearby, were sceptical but some "witnesses" spoke of beings in silvery suits . . .

"Oh, those arrived three years ago, but then we've always had a lot of Yanks stationed round here!"

"That must have been a rehearsal we saw on Sunday."

Neil Kinnock, in Brighton for the Labour Party conference, slipped into the sea and was grabbed by his wife—photographers just happened to be there at the time.

Elsie Tanner (leaving *Coronation Street*), Geoff Boycott (sacked by Yorkshire) gave newspapers and magazines ample scope for comment and speculation. Boycott, to many cricket fans' relief, stayed on.

"Have you got something without Elsie Tanner or Geoff Boycott in it?"

Cabinet Minister Cecil Parkinson admitted that his former secretary was expecting his baby.

"<u>Y</u>ou can cross Cecil Parkinson off the queer list, sir!"

A Young Tories' report said that extreme Right-wingers were infiltrating the Conservative Party.

JAK

"This is my son Rodney, Eton, Cambridge, and prospective candidate for Westminster!"

The Opposition were being thoroughly gentlemanly and reticent about the Parkinson affair . . .

"I must say it's been jolly decent of the Opposition not to cash in on the 'Parky' scandal!"

"**Finally, Norman, I'd like you to take a little test!**"

Norman Tebbit took over from Cecil Parkinson at the Department of Trade and Industry.

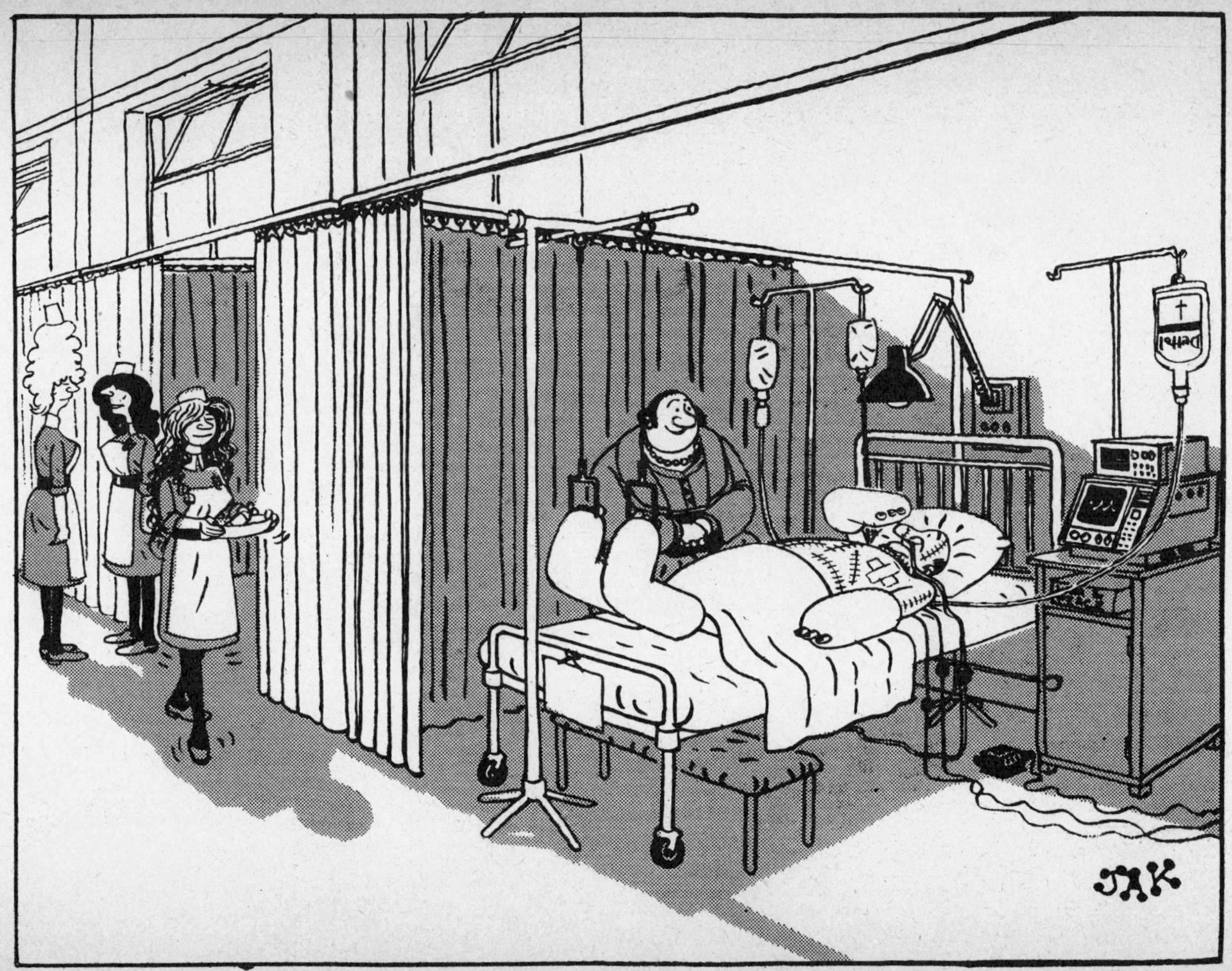

A hairdresser posed as a doctor in several London hospitals and even helped qualified staff without arousing suspicion. At last someone queried his qualifications and he was exposed, charged and held for psychiatric reports.

"Mind you he's given you a terrific haircut!"

The two policemen who shot Stephen Waldorf, mistaking him for the wanted criminal David Martin, were cleared on self-defence grounds.

" Don't worry, sir, they only issue them to police marksmen ! "

More and more newspapers were giving their readers the chance to win big money prizes.

"Scroggins! Are you going in for every blasted newspaper competition?"

A Welsh solicitor was found guilty of over-charging his clients by some £100,000.

"Then Snodgrass overcharged Davies who was then overcharged by Mullins, who was then overcharged by Hardcastle and Longbridge, who were . . . !"

Cubans building an airport in Grenada were offering surprising resistance to the American invasion force.

"If you want to muck about Mulligan, do it in your own time!"

Greenham Common women used wire cutters to get into the base and were arrested.

"**Sorry, miss. Somebody must have taken down the sign!**"

Myra, a police dog that tackled soccer hooligans, was given the Police Dog Action of the Year award and attended the Men of the Year lunch at the Savoy Hotel.

"I don't know how you did it chef but they're all raving about your Pedigree Chum!"

"I think we'll need an elephant gun for this one, sarge!"

Mr Heseltine, the Defence Minister, would not confirm an allegation that protestors who broke into Greenham Common air base would be shot at.

The man who pretended to be a doctor was not imprisoned but sent for treatment.

"Next!!"

The release by the Home Office of the Oswald Mosley papers revealed various people and organisations who had given support to the British Union of Fascists in the 1930s.

"**Bang goes your story about being a Dorset fruit farmer during the 30's, Algy !**"

A couple decided that a light plane at Luton airport would be ideal to make love in . . . it was on the ground at the time.

"I don't know who's giving that girl a lesson, but I haven't seen manoeuvres like that since the Battle of Britain."

Red paint was thrown at
Mr Heseltine when he
tried to address students
at Manchester University.

"There must have been a defoliant in that paint, Michael."

Parliament agreed that UHT milk and frozen cream could be imported from France under EEC regulations.

" Mind you, the wife liked it daily !"

How a familiar French tradesman might modernise his business ideas thanks to the EEC.

A report on the Metropolitan Police accused them, among other things, of being racist and far from the image of the helpful local Bobby.

"Kind ! Considerate ! Teetotal ! He'll never get anywhere in the police !"

British Rail tried out a cheaper type of rolling-stock on one route. Comfort was not the first consideration.

"Excuse me! Is this third class?"

Four new prisons are to be built in well-populated areas—one at Milton Keynes, for example.

"Has he told you where the new prison's going?"

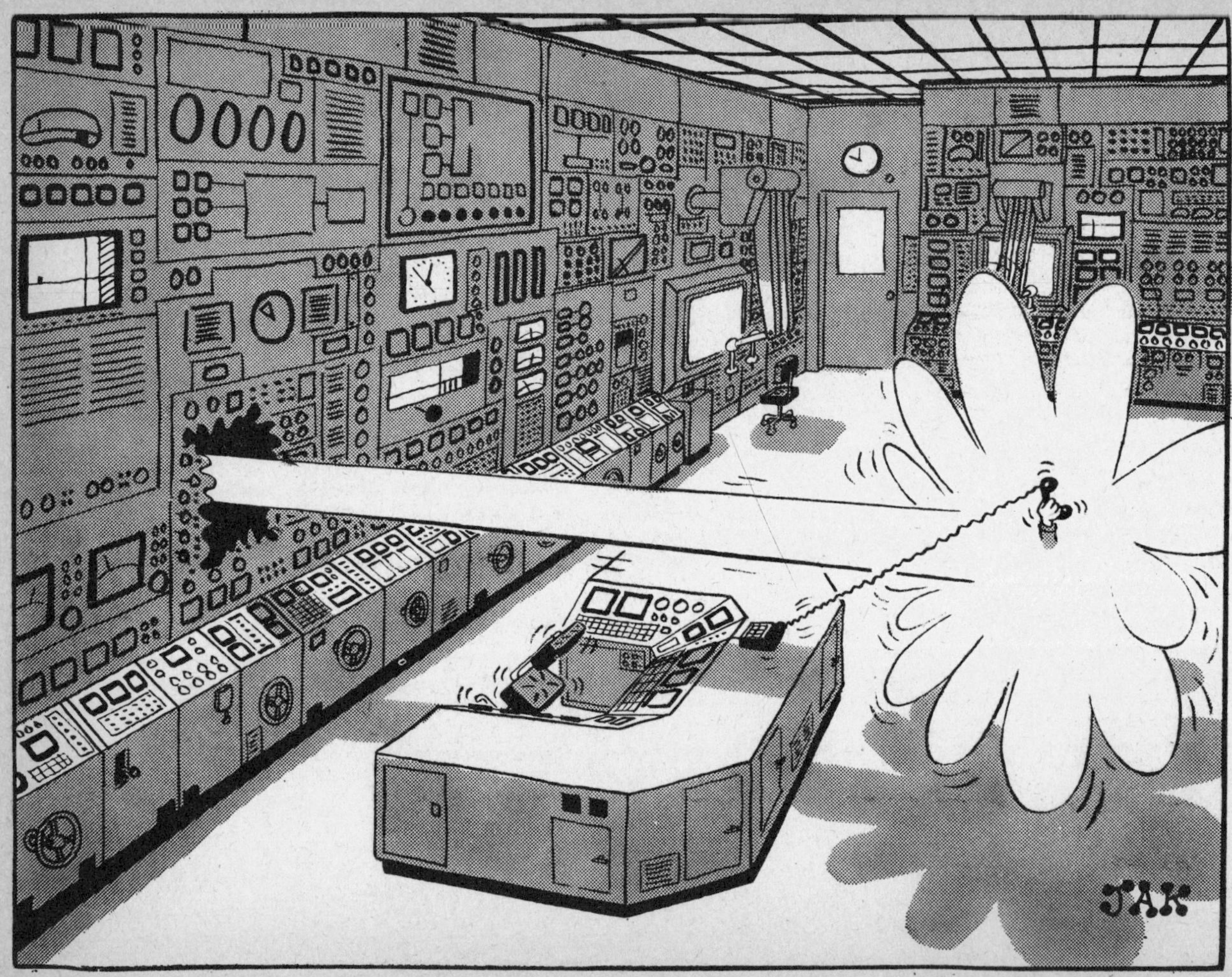

British Nuclear Fuels foiled an attempt by Green Peace to block the nuclear outfall into the sea off Sellafield, formerly known as Windscale.

"Hello! Control here! I think Greenpeace have found the plug hole!"

A survey alleged that an alarmingly high percentage of young children had seen video nasties.

"Mum! Dad! You can come in now. The video nasty's finished!"

"I don't know if it's of any help in your inquiries inspector, but we had six nasty cases of hernia admitted last night!"

A huge quantity of gold bars were stolen from a security warehouse near Heathrow.

Parliament ruled that opticians no longer had the monopoly to supply spectacles.

"Shorry, offisher! It must have been my high street spectacles!"

So many names, so many factions: the conflict in Lebanon became increasingly complicated.

HMS *Invincible* was not allowed into an Australian dry dock for repairs because the captain would not say whether nuclear weapons were on board or not.

"A splendid job men! Now, let's have another go at getting in!"

Sean Connery, not in the first flush of youth, returned to active screen duty as Agent 007.

"They say the wheelchair chase is fantastic!"

To celebrate their 50th anniversary, the Cumberland Hotel adorned their façade with a model of King Kong, also 50 years old this year.

"Your gorilla has just eaten my doorman!"

A policewoman told to move from motor patrol duty because her superiors thought she might have an affair with her married policeman partner won a sex discrimination case against the Police.

"Do you mind if we stop off at my house? I'd like to reassure my wife!"

To the embarrassment of the Irish police, searching for the chief of the Irish National Liberation Army, some of their officers were held up and had to hand over their uniforms and identity cards.

"Irish police are closing in on Dominic McGlinchy!"

"A train set! A train set! You'll have a ⋯⋯ computer like everyone else"

The day Father Christmas
met an old-fashioned child . . .

After an IRA bomb had caused deaths and injuries at Harrods, West End stores took extra precautions.

"Hardcastle! Hardcastle! I don't think we need a complete body search of everybody!"

"We caught this one trying to make a run for it, inspector!"

Police in force raided what was rumoured to be a "gambling den" at
Hove but found an old folks' club peacefully playing bridge.
There were no prosecutions . . .

While the Royal Family were enjoying their New Year shoot at Sandringham, the Queen asked Press photographers to stop being so attentive.

"Not terribly good so far Charles—just a brace of freelance photographers!"

British Rail issued Timex watches to drivers as an aid to efficiency.

"No wonder you're late. You've got the big hand pointing to Mickey Mouse's left ear!"

In the highly successful *Thorn Birds* series on BBC TV, Richard Chamberlain played a priest strongly tempted by feminine charms.

"I saw it too, so it looks like 10 Hail Mary's for both of us !"

The Far Pavilions and *The Jewel in the Crown* on TV were reviving memories of the British in India.

"I shall be glad when all this blasted Indian television stuff is over!"

"We couldn't find a French lorry driver!"

A former research laboratory in Teddington was found to have traces of radiation—not dangerous as it turned out.

"Of course, there's a slight radiation risk!"

The high price of housebuilding in the Falklands was revealed when it came to providing accommodation for British military personnel.

"Of course, if it was in Mayfair it would be half the price."

Linda McCartney was fined £75 for having cannabis in her luggage at Heathrow.

"It's not the usual poppy colonel, these you roll up and smoke."

President Reagan announced he would be running for a second term —at the end of it he would be in his late seventies.

"It's Shirley Temple, Mr President, she wants to be an Ambassador again!"

A young jockey was banned for three years for taking a bribe from a gambler.

" All right, I'll come clean. He made me do it !"

In fact Nissan eventually decided to establish their new car plant at Washington New Town on Wearside.

"What happens if Nissan don't build it around here, Dai?"

English sport at a low ebb —they lost to New Zealand at cricket by an innings and were beaten by the Scots Rugby XV at Murrayfield.

"Henry! Which one is that Geoffrey Howe in charge of, GCHQ, GLC, MCC or the RFC?"

French farmers were holding up foreign meat lorries in yet another protest.

"Did you hear the joke about the Irish lorry driver who nearly fooled the French

Some British residents were being taken out of war-ravaged Beirut by car ferry.

"I'm afraid you've left it a bit late for the duty-free shop, sir!"

Labour leader Neil Kinnock's trip to the United States had aroused little attention; the England cricket team had lost their series in New Zealand.

"I'm not sure if it's the welcome-back party for the England cricket team or for Neil Kinnock!"

Protesting over hold-ups at Italian Customs, French lorry drivers were blocking many roads on the Continent.

"Well, what is it sunshine, a jack-knife, or a protest?"

Prince Andrew had a new girl-friend . . .

"Do you remember when it was a nice quiet middle class neighbourhood!"

Jimmy Savile became a member of the exclusive Athenaeum Club.

"Jim fixed it for him!"

At the Government Communications HQ, Cheltenham, March 1 was the deadline for obeying the Government's order to give up union membership and take the £1,000 offered.

"Next!!"

Virgin Records went into the airline business offering cheap transatlantic fares.

"We're having a hell of a job finding a qualified air hostess!"

An official report confirmed the high number of children who had seen videos not meant for their impressionable little minds . . .

" . . . And finally, have you noticed any change in Harold since he started watching video nasties ?"

The new machine having proved temperamental, another possible way to test motorists under the influence . . .

"I said! Would you put this in your ear and blow into it?"

Even a skilful motorist can lose his head sometimes . . .

"I think you did most of the damage when you ran over your mother-in-law the eighth time!"

The Queen began her royal tour of Jordan amid strict security.

"Too noisy at the Iranian Embassy! Too cold in the Falklands! Sometimes I wonder why you lot joined the SAS!"

That intoximeter was giving unreliable results so it was decided that a suspect could opt for alternative methods . . .

"Right! All together now, three, two, one . . . !"

Baliffs moved the Greenham Camp women to make way for a road widening project.

"Are you sure you moved all the peace women, Murphy?"

Some TV series grip more than others . . .

"Doris has taken the ending of ' The Jewel in the Crown ' very badly !"

Michael Bettaney, an MI5 man who tried unsuccessfully to become a Russian spy—they weren't interested—was jailed for 23 years.

"I'm afraid we're in for another ghastly scandal.   We've discovered a chap in MI5 working for the British!"

Mrs Thatcher announced her intention of leading the Tories at the next election.

The Labour Party is not amused !

During the Libyan embassy siege, with Police barriers round the square, some workers got to their offices via the rooftops.

"You don't have to come to the office that way any more, Mrs Gibbs!"

British women workers in Iranian banks in this country were told to conform with Iranian standards of modesty in their dress.

"I only work in the bank part-time!"

The London Marathon on May 13 attracted the usual huge entry of game runners, some fit and many who thought they were.

"Eighteen hours, ten minutes. I'm sure he wants to thank you for suggesting he ran in the marathon!"

The Princess of Wales's brother, Viscount Althorp, and some friends tried to debag disc jockey Tony Blackburn in a London restaurant.

"By the way, Mr Blackburn, service wasn't included!"

Miners' leader Arthur Scargill accused Police of jostling him on a picket line.

" And this is a demonstration of the correct way to push Arthur Scargill ! "

Having established Irish family connections to his own satisfaction, President Reagan visited Ireland.

"They're tossing up to decide who holds you upside down while you kiss the Blarney Stone!"

A nurse who posed for a nude centrefold was sacked.

We'll have to wait for next week's issue. They could only get one half of Nurse Winterbottom on the centrefold!"

Francis Pym, former Foreign Secretary, criticised Mrs Thatcher in his new book.

"Of course ma'am, if Mr Pym's fingernails grow again, he could be signing copies of his book by Christmas!"

Smoking was to be banned completely on the London Underground.

"He was gasping for a fag!"

It was reported that Prince Andrew had gone with a party of friends to a restaurant where people who hanker after school food and discipline can be catered for.

" Of course, on the à la carte menu you could have two lovely black eyes from the chef!"

A vet hit the headlines when he helped a surgeon to perform an operation.

"Bring him back on Friday and I'll take the stitches out!"

The men alleged to have carried out several big bullion robberies were said to be living in luxury in Spain, with whom Britain has no extradition treaty.

"Sometimes I miss the Old Kent Road — but not that much!"

Gipsies arrived to camp on Hampstead Heath and among the protesters was Michael Foot, who takes his dog Dizzy for walks there.

"Not that old tramp over there, **THAT** old tramp over there!"

Lightning was thought to be responsible for the partial destruction of York Minster's south transept.

"Put that fag out, vicar, here comes the man from the insurance!"

Banks put up interest by two per cent, building societies warned of impending mortgage rises, the Government ban on trade unions at the GCHQ, Cheltenham, was ruled illegal by the High Court—it was not one of Mrs Thatcher's best weeks . . .

". . . And now to complete Mrs Thatcher's week, she will be attacked by three dozen RAF police dogs and the massed bands of the Royal Marines!"